The Future of
the Corporation

Michael Novak

The AEI Press

Publisher for the American Enterprise Institute

WASHINGTON, D.C.

1996

Distributed to the Trade by National Book Network, 15200 NBN Way, Blue Ridge Summit, PA 17214. To order call toll free 1-800-462-6420 or 1-717-794-3800. For all other inquiries please contact the AEI Press, 1150 Seventeenth Street, N.W., Washington, D.C. 20036 or call 1-800-862-5801.

ISBN 0-8447-7080-9
ISBN 978-0-8447-7080-2
1 3 5 7 9 10 8 6 4 2

THE AEI PRESS
Publisher for the American Enterprise Institute
1150 17th Street, N.W., Washington, D.C. 20036

The Corporation, as we know it—and we know it from every aspect of our lives—was invented; it did not come to be of itself.

OSCAR HANDLIN

The Future of
the Corporation

Contents

Preface

In the summer of 1995, representatives of Pfizer Inc. approached me about preparing three lectures on key issues facing business corporations as the new century approaches. At first I was hesitant to set aside a book project already begun, but since I was free to choose topics and approach, I agreed to return to terrain I had explored in the 1980s on the nature of the corporation in *The Corporation: A Theoretical Inquiry* and *Toward a Theology of the Corporation*.

Much has changed in the intervening years. A renewed account of the corporation seemed useful: what the corporation is, its new moral challenges and the new enemies it faces, and what goods (and dangers) it brings with it. This monograph on the future of the corporation is the first in a series of three Pfizer Lectures, which will be published over the next few months. The second will explore intellectual property and human creativity; and the third, crucial aspects of corporate governance.

I would like to thank Pfizer Inc. for its support, and in particular Terry Gallagher and Carson Daly. In my own office, Cathie Love and Brian Anderson carried on with their usual competence and unusual good cheer. Permit me to thank AEI, too, which under the watchful eye of Chris DeMuth continues to provide a remarkably welcome home for research and writing; Isabel Ferguson and Ethel Dailey in the office of Seminars and Conferences, who arranged the public presentation on May 21, 1996; and Dana Lane, who showed tender care in the supervision of this publication.

The Future of the Corporation

T he war of 1848–1989 between capitalism and socialism is over; capitalism has won.[1] As an *economic* idea, socialism has been defeated. As a *political* idea, socialism lives.

Almost everywhere, from Chile to Britain, Socialists have openly embraced private market economies, innovation, enterprise, and economic growth, but they have not ceased being Socialists. They have not ceased hating capitalism or assaulting Thatcherism and Reaganism.

Nor have they ceased identifying their primordial enemy as the private business corporation. They no longer speak of replacing the "anarchy" of markets with national planning, of nationalizing private industries, or of confiscating profits. Today they speak of environmentalism, of education, of enhancing human capital, and—to tame their chief nemesis and rival—of corporate responsibility and corporate governance.

Without going so far as the British journalist Will Hutton and his big book of 1995, *The State We're In,*[2]

head of the Labour Party Tony Blair has recently an-
nounced his "big idea" for Britain's future: "the Stakeholder Society." *Stakeholder* is intended as a contrast
to *shareholder*. Hutton's new big idea is in effect to turn
business corporations into adjuncts of the welfare
state, in which every citizen of Britain has a stake and
on which each citizen has a claim. Everyone in Britain will be a stakeholder. The whole island will "re-
gain" the feeling of belonging to a great family with
a corporate purpose and corporate pride. The wal-
lets of shareholders will, of course, be open to other
stakeholders.

This is but one example of the new ethos into
which the business corporation, like a proud and full-
sailed man-o'-war flush with victory, is unguardedly
sailing. Another example, closer to home, appears in
Newsweek's cover story, "Corporate Killers," featur-
ing mug shots of four chief executive officers.[3] American business, in particular, is being rudely awakened,
just at a moment of triumph.

From having been universally mocked as recently as five years ago for falling behind the Japanese and the European Community, American business (manufacturing, in particular) has once again
become celebrated for being the world's leader, the
system most to be studied and imitated.

Having been accused of being too blinkered by
the drive for short-term performance, it has again
seized the lead in fields of long-term significance such
as biotechnology, telecommunications, and the
Internet, in all of which the enormous long-range investments undertaken in the 1980s are at last coming
to fruition. And significant productivity increases are

beginning to show up in the rapidly expanding service sector, as well.

So why, then, the current rude awakening?

The Achilles' heel of American corporations has been a lack of ideological self-consciousness. Business leaders underestimate the size, intensity, intelligence, and commitment of the forces determined to undermine corporate independence.

Making a business work is not a merely theoretical matter; it takes a tough, confident, and pragmatic mind. Yet in these days of instant communications and easy demagoguery, corporate leaders who lack an unclouded philosophical picture of where they and their opponents stand have too weak a radar to detect the threats arrayed against them. Pragmatism today demands philosophical sophistication. The new sin against pragmatism is to be ideologically naked against determined enemies.

Recently, for example, several British companies signed off on an assertion that

> those companies which will sustain competitive success in the future are those which focus less exclusively on shareholders and financial measures of performance—and instead include all their stakeholder relationships in the way they think and talk about their purpose and performance.

Do the executives of NatWest, Cadbury Schweppes, Guinness, Midland Electricity, Unipart, and other signatories of this report (ominously called "Tomorrow's Company") truly believe that shareholders around the world will continue to invest in companies that

so diffuse their purposes? No doubt, being pragmatic
gentlemen, they intend to grant the opposition a victory in rhetoric, while afterwards hoping to muddle
through more or less as always. One does have the
eerie feeling, though, that British companies are let-
ting themselves be led to slaughter like British cattle.
Alas, American executives also sign grand manifes-
toes on the environment and other pieties, thus com-
mitting acts of ideological appeasement that in politicians they would speedily denounce.

It is necessary to begin by going back to basics.

What Is a Corporation?

*No single factor describes why capitalism
emerged; . . . as well as geography, technology
and Christianity, a particular form of political
and economic system was needed, [which] con-
tained an implicit separation between economic
and political power, between the market and government.*

ALAN MACFARLANE
The Culture of Capitalism[4]

In the most recent figures (1995), there were nearly 11
million business corporations in the United States,
approximately one for every twelve workers.[5] They
cover a vast range of types. Some of them are only
one-person professional corporations. Some are independent franchises of large chains such as
McDonald's, Tastee Freez, Kentucky Fried Chicken,
and True Value Hardware. Others are auto
dealerships or owners of buildings. One of the larg-

est sources of U.S. jobs, the construction industry (employing 4.5 million), is divided into nearly 600,000 different firms, often involved in quite strenuous local competition and in many market niches. Nearly four thousand business corporations are publicly traded companies, most (but not all) listed on the New York, American, or NASDAQ stock exchanges; these are the companies on which we shall concentrate.

A notable fact about the largest and most famous corporations, the *Fortune* 500 and the *Forbes* 400, is that they now employ only a little over 9 percent of all U.S. employees, whereas twenty years ago they employed nearly 19 percent (in 1975, 16 million out of 86 million jobs). This decline occurred both because the U.S. economy has created some 37 million new jobs since 1975 and because the largest corporations have shed nearly 4.5 million jobs (from about 16 million to about 11.5 million). Sometimes this shedding happens because firms new to the top 400 or 500—such as Microsoft (9,000 employees)—employ as many as 100,000 fewer workers than those they replace.[6]

Thus, the corporation, legally considered, is a magnificent social invention, prior in its existence to the modern nation-state. The laws governing corporations appear to go back in their origin to ancient Egyptian burial societies and, in the Christian West, to religious monasteries, towns, and universities. Such legally constituted societies possessed an independence recognized by successive political regimes. Their independence from the state had a legitimacy implicitly founded in primeval rights of association and common respect for the sacred. Such institutions were constituted to endure beyond the lifetimes of their founding generation.

The founder of Western monasticism, St. Benedict (480–547), having learned from the early Christian hermitages in Egypt, wisely provided for regular and frequent changes of leadership in each monastery according to formal rules. He staked out unsettled and often remote lands on which the economic sustainability, however meager, of each new foundation could be ensured for generations.

Among historians, it is no longer unusual to suggest that the Benedictine (and other) monasteries sweeping north into Europe from Italy and east from Ireland, gradually beginning to sell their wines, cheeses, brandies, and breads from region to region, were the West's first transnational corporations. The monks introduced to many formerly nomadic peoples what was, for its time, scientific agriculture, thus enabling entire regions to advance beyond subsistence living. From the surplus thus accumulated, libraries and schools, music halls and commissions for paintings grew; civilization took root. Arts and sciences such as botany, metallurgy, and architecture were nourished, and industries such as mining and engineering were furthered. As the historian Paul Johnson has described it:

> A great and increasing part of the arable land of Europe passed into the hands of highly disciplined men committed to a doctrine of hard work. They were literate. They knew how to keep accounts. Above all, perhaps, they worked to a daily timetable and an ac-

curate annual calendar—something quite alien to the farmers and landowners they replaced. Thus their cultivation of the land was organized, systematic, persistent. And, as owners, they escaped the accidents of deaths, minorities, administration by hapless widows, enforced sales, or transfer of ownership by crime, treason and folly. They brought continuity of exploitation. They produced surpluses and invested them in the form of drainage, clearances, livestock and seed . . . they determined the whole future history of Europe; they were the foundation of its world primacy.[7]

Thus, contemporary studies of economic history push the origins of capitalism, especially in its underlying institutional forms and laws, back into monastic history, the transnational sensibility of the Christian faith, and the vigorous (if sometimes misguided and invariably controversial) efforts of the papacy to maintain, even by force of military might, the common trade routes and civilizational ties of a united Europe. It is not by accident that the Medal of Europe, awarded annually for contributions to European civilization, bears the embossed portrait of St. Benedict.

Under Islam, by contrast, it is not easy to maintain a separation of church and state; it seems to be part of the essence of Islam, in some sense, to insist on unity. Islam calls for a sort of integrism of faith and life foreign to American Protestantism—but also foreign to medieval Catholicism. When St. Ambrose of Milan (340–397) forbade the soldiers of Emperor

Theodosius to enter his cathedral, and they obeyed, he was marking off the boundaries of civil society— in this case, the church—across which the state dared not intrude.[8] In an analogous way, other corporations of civil society appealed to legal precedents, traditions, and principles to defend their own independence from soldiers of the regime, tyrants, and armed bullies who coveted their goods. Often rights *were* lost, injustices *were* done, and right had to be revindicated by force of arms or after the passage of evil times. But a sense of the limits of the state gradually took hold, and with it, the preeminence of the institutions of civil society over those of the state.

Ancient charters, privileges once conferred for exceptional services, exemptions hard won, freedoms achieved, rights recognized by successive regimes, custom, tradition, precedent—in all these, great social power long dwelt. By their means, as well as by experiment, observation, and the common sense of things, the common law developed, especially in Britain. Friedrich Hayek argues that by this evolutionary path the principles of the market economy were learned "not through the design of some wise legislator but through a process of trial and error,"[9] thick with the experience of daily life.

Surely, this is how individual markets grew— among weapons makers, how practitioners came to recognize, for example, good metal from poor, real craftsmanship from shoddy, superior technologies from inferior, models of stunning proportion and form from those merely useful. Tacit rules grew up in such individual markets concerning certain practices that were unacceptable, certain materials beneath approved standards, certain designs recognized as faulty.

Over time, and especially closer to our own time, discoveries such as double-entry bookkeeping, the stock association, mutual insurance societies, the beginnings of organizational theory, patent and copyright arrangements, the power of newly invented machines, and the possibilities of large-scale and mass production opened up new horizons for the business corporation.

Capping these historical developments, the Japanese sociologist Kazua Noda writes:

> The corporate form itself developed in the early Middle Ages with the growth and codification of civil and canon law. . . . The first corporations were towns, universities, and ecclesiastical orders. They differed from partnerships in that the organization existed independently of any particular membership; but they were not, like modern business corporations, the "property" of their participants. . . . By the 15th century, the courts of England had agreed on the principle of "limited liability": "If something is owed to the group, it is not owed to the individuals nor do the individuals owe what the group owes." . . . As applied later to stockholders in business corporations [this principle] served to encourage investment because the most an individual could lose in the event of the firm's failure would be the actual amount he originally paid for his shares.[10]

Business corporations—either independent of the state or commissioned by the state (the latter at first more common)—were designed to continue beyond the life of the founding generation, began to provide goods and services on a scale theretofore unseen, and needed vast amounts of human and financial capital. These voluntary associations had to prove themselves, often against quite entrenched opposition from the social classes they threatened (the landed aristocracy, for example). And yet, as Karl Marx noted, they transformed the world. They were indispensable to making it free and prosperous. Yet from the beginning, long before Marx appeared on the scene, business corporations had enemies.

For centuries, men of commerce had been ill thought of by farmers and fishermen, landowners, aristocrats, churchmen, poets, and philosophers— seen as pursuers of mammon, middlemen who bought cheap and sold dear, sophisticates and cheats, hucksters, admirers not of the noble but the merely useful, men with the souls of slaves, cosmopolitans without loyalties. The counts against them are as old as portions of the Bible, Plato and Aristotle, Horace and Cicero.[11] Aristocrats most businessmen certainly were not. It is a curious but also crucial fact that men of business have been morally assaulted, for many generations now, both by the aristocratic and the humanistic Right and by the modern Socialist, social democratic, and merely progovernmental Left. Elites on both sides denounce them, chiefly on moral (but also on aesthetic) grounds. When critics reluctantly discover that most of what businessmen do is legal and moral, and even useful, they retreat to thinking it unlovely. Anticapitalism is a far, far darker dye than socialism, and harder to remove.

While it is true that business leaders have few pretensions of being aristocrats or literary intellectuals or social reformers—not, at least, through their work in business—it is important to say that business is a morally serious calling. Through business you can do great good or great evil, and all the variations on the scale. But if you do good, you have the advantage that it is the design of business as a practice and as an institution that you do so;[12] whereas if you do evil, it is because you have twisted a good thing to your own evil purposes and have no one to blame but yourself. The market may make you or break you, favor your new product or leave it on the shelf—the market does not smile on everyone alike—but in moral matters one is never in a position to say, "The market made me do it." You did it. You are the agent in the market; the market is no agent.

In the early Middle Ages, in sum, the corporation began as burial societies, then monasteries and towns and universities. Implicitly rooted in rights of association, the corporation was "an instrument of privilege and a kind of exclusive body, tightly controlled by the state for reasons of its own."[13] But, as Oscar Handlin points out, in the infant United States there was great resistance to dependence on royal charters from far across the ocean and a great desire among citizens to form corporations on their own to meet innumerable needs. The citizens of Massachusetts, for example, as early as 1636 made up a charter of incorporation for Harvard University, much to the shock of violated royal prerogative on the other side of the

Atlantic. Thus, by 1750, while England still had but
two universities, the American colonies had six. By
1880, there were more universities in the state of Ohio
than in all of Europe combined. Similarly, the railroad had been invented in England, but ten years later
there were more miles of railroad in the United States
than in all of Britain—and all of Europe—combined.[14]
When American lawyers did not even know how to
write up proper incorporation papers, they nonetheless did so, and business corporations multiplied up
and down the Eastern seaboard. As Handlin has writ-
ten:

> In 1800 the United States was only begin-
> ning its history as an independent nation. It
> was an underdeveloped country, primarily
> agricultural, with a population of perhaps 4
> or 5 million along the Atlantic coast. Already,
> however, the United States had more cor-
> porations, and more explicitly business cor-
> porations, than all of Europe put together;
> this is an astounding circumstance if you
> look at it from the point of view of the econo-
> mist.

Thus, in the United States, the business corporation
came into its independent own. Here were born the
very first manufacturing corporations in the world.[15]
Here corporations ceased being based on state privilege, monopoly, trust, or grant and became inventions
of civil society and independent citizens. The state
retained a right to *approve of* applications and to reg-
ister them, for good legal order, but it did not create a
right or convey its own power to the corporation or

guarantee the latter's survival. The corporation, to survive, could no longer depend on its privileges; it could survive only if it met the needs of its customers and the purposes of its investors. It brought to civil society not only independence from the state but also unparalleled social flexibility and a zest for risk and dare.

Thus, the business corporation grows out of a long, worthy, and civilizing history. It is a voluntary association committed to a common enterprise—an enterprise association, as Michael Oakeshott would call it[16]—that consists in providing particular goods or services to the larger human community, either to the whole world or to one or more of its smaller communities. The business corporation springs from the creative act of its founders, who are usually moved by a new invention or idea to provide to a particular market something otherwise unavailable, or not available in the unique form in which they have presented it. Their aim is to provide this good or service at a price attractive to potential customers, in the hope of making a sustainable profit over time.

This hope of a reasonable return on their investment attracts investors to join their funds to the purposes of the firm. As Peter Drucker has pointed out, in our time shareholders play a more transient role in the corporation than they have in the past; but for any growing, creative, and self-transforming firm, new shareholders willing to invest remain important members of the business corporation:

> Though we have largely abandoned it in legal and political practice, the old crude fic-

tion still lingers on which regards the corporation as nothing but the sum of the property rights of the individual shareholders.
Thus, for instance, the president of a company will report to the shareholders on the
state of "their" company. In this conven-
tional formula the corporation is seen as
transitory and as existing only by virtue of
a legal fiction while the shareholder is re-
garded as permanent and actual. In the social reality of today, however, shareholders
are but one of several groups of people who
stand in a special relationship to the corporation. The corporation is permanent, the
shareholder is transitory. It might even be
said without much exaggeration that the
corporation is really socially and politically
a priori whereas the shareholder's position
is derivative and exists only in contempla-
tion of law.[17]

Will Hutton's view notwithstanding, the shareholder,
however indispensable, is far from the center of things
and is likely to be as diffused throughout civil society as the holders of pension funds.

The Corporation and Civil Society

From the point of view of civil society, the business
enterprise is an important social good for four reasons. First, it creates jobs. Second, it provides desir-
able goods and services. Third, through its profits it
creates wealth that did not exist before. And fourth,
it is a private social instrument, independent of the

state, for the moral and material support of other activities of civil society.

In recent decades, this last-mentioned independence from the state has been more and more compromised, through "command and control" regulations and heavy-handed "guidance" from ambitious politicians, promiscuous with state and federal power. Not surprisingly, economic growth has been grinding to slow, fitful levels. And the iron of state programs is rubbing through the fabric of civil society.

Alexis de Tocqueville wrote that religion is the first political institution of civil society.[18] No doubt, Tocqueville had in mind the importance of the truths enunciated by Judaism and Christianity concerning the immortal value of every single person and the crucial role of truth (that is, the opposite of relativism) in making possible the reasoned discourse on which civilization depends. In the opening lines of *Federalist* No.1, Alexander Hamilton appeals to the capacities of his readers for reasoned argument, pointing out that the upcoming vote on the new Constitution will afford a test of whether, for the first time in history, a nation can be founded not on force or chance, but on reflection and choice.[19] Apart from a prior commitment to truth, no such reflection and reasoned argument are possible; nor is it possible to defend claims to the imperishable rights of humans. (For to claims made on the basis of relativism, not truth, an objector may retort, "That's just your opinion.") To put Tocqueville's point in a contemporary idiom, religious liberty is the first of all human rights, for it implies the dignity and sacredness of human conscience.

Nonetheless, in another sense business is also the first political institution of civil society. Our founders believed it to be part of their originality to establish here a "commercial republic,"[20] because they believed that a republic finds a safer foundation on commerce than on the aristocracy, religion, or the military. A commercial republic has its own temptations, of course, of which neither they nor Tocqueville was unaware (see *Federalist* No.6). But temptations inherent in other possible foundations are far more dangerous and lack compensating advantages. Following Montesquieu, they held that commerce inherently cries out for law and teaches respect for law; benefits by peace and is destroyed by war; teaches prudence and attention to small losses and small gains; softens manners; diverts attention from issues of glory and spiritual divisiveness to seek modest progress on humble but useful matters; and distributes the practical interests of people, even in the same families, among different industries and different firms.[21]

This last contribution, in turn, affords two advantages: it teaches people even in the same family to understand different occupations, interests, and points of view and how to accommodate them, and it makes it socially far more difficult to form a tyrannical majority. Our founders well knew that the greatest of all tyrants is not a single ruler but an unchecked majority. Democracies in the past, they knew, most often fell because of the tyranny of a majority, and this fate they were committed, by as many remedies as possible, to prevent. The promotion of manufacturing and commerce was a most central and important preventive measure.

Moreover, sources of private capital and private wealth, independent of the state, are crucial to the survival of liberty. The alternative is dependence on government, the opposite of liberty. The chief funder of the many works of civil society, from hospitals and research institutes to museums, the opera, orchestras, and universities is the business corporation. The corporation today is even a major funder of public television. Absent the financial resources of major corporations, civil society would be a poor thing, indeed.

Pittsburgh, Chicago, New York, Boston, Tulsa, San Francisco, and other American cities—without the philanthropic habits of their corporate leaders over many generations—would be culturally and aesthetically far less pleasing than they are. Most of the buildings on our college and university campuses, even those that are part of state systems, were funded by private donors. What at Oxford and Cambridge monarchs and princes have done is done in America by men and women of business. People in other countries, lacking such traditions, have no way of envisioning the civic leadership, cultural imagination, and immense benefactions contributed by business firms to American life. The magnitude of business and other private giving to colleges and universities in America has no parallel on this planet.

Finally, it should be observed that the ownership of publicly owned companies extends through more than half the American adult population. The largest holders of stocks and bonds are the pension plans of workers, in the public sector as well as the private sector. To cite just two examples, TIAA-CREF, the pension plan of educators, researchers, and university staffs, as of the end of 1995 owned over $69 billion in stocks and bonds, and the pension plan of the public employees of California owned over $50 billion.

More than 51 million Americans, in addition to those who own stock through pension funds, also own stock either directly or through their personal mutual funds, IRAs, and defined-contribution pension plans. Total stock owned directly by individuals at the end of 1995 was worth $3.6 trillion.[22] Seventy percent of families owning such stock have annual incomes under $75,000. Even apart from new investments, current funds may be expected to grow, on average, at about 8 percent a year. The independence of families from government is closely tied to such investments.

If in the near future social security is privatized, pouring multiple billions of dollars of new funds into productive investment, the independence of individual families will be mightily fortified. Shareholders are no small, narrow band of the American population but a large majority.

Business corporations are crucial institutions of civil society—they support research, the arts, universities, charities, and good works of many kinds, and they undergird the financial hopes of American families. Above all, they expand the space for independence and private action in the public sphere. They add greatly to the diversity of sources of public imagination, initiative, and experimentation.

The Stakeholder Society

From these reflections it is obvious that the business corporation is indispensable to the maintenance of any true experiment in self-government. It plays a crucial role in the design of the republican experiment—it is the commercial part of the commercial republic, the principal economic part of political economy. In that sense, then, all citizens of the republic have a *stake* in the success and vitality of American corporations. From these derive Americans' financial independence from government and their practical freedom of action.

Here a fateful equivocation must be cleared up. The word *stakeholder* has two senses. The term derives from the time of the Homestead Act, when Americans heading West could take out a claim on a parcel of land and be guaranteed the ownership thereof by the protection of the state.[23] The federal government sponsored this act for two reasons: first, to make sure that the West developed as free states, not slave states, and second, to reap the benefits of a regime of private ownership and private practical intelligence. At that time, Americans believed (in lessons derived from the experience of ancient Rome and Greece as well as from medieval Europe and Britain) that the common good is better served by a regime of private property than by common ownership or state ownership. They further believed that more intelligence springs from a multitude of practical-minded owners of their own property than from a prestigious body of planners, however brilliant. Iowa, in effect, would develop with more practical good sense under scores of thousands of small owners than under a plantation system such as that of the South or some scheme of state planning.

In this context, *stakeholder* means *owner* and pri-

vate *risk taker*. The purpose of an arrangement of society into many private stakeholders is to secure the
general welfare and the larger *public* interest. The stakeholder society in this sense is the very foundation of
the free society. Maintaining it entails investment,
hard work, responsibility, risk, and earned reward or,
often enough, personal failure. Freedom is tied to risk
and responsibility.

The social democratic sense of the term *stakeholder*
is quite different. Stakeholders are all those who deem
themselves entitled to make demands on the system
and to receive from it. A Britain, for example, imagined as a "stakeholder society" is one in which each
citizen is entitled to make claims on others according
to his or her needs. These needs are infinitely expan-
sive, however, so perpetual dissatisfaction is guaranteed. No conceivable amount of security or health care
can satisfy human beings; our longings are infinite,
beyond all earthly satisfaction. If today's ten most
dangerous diseases are conquered, the next ten will
rise to cause new anxiety. A stakeholder society is
bound to be like a nest of open-mouthed chicks. The
link between the desire to receive and personal responsibility never forms.

The social democratic dream has many of the
characteristics of a religion. It is, in particular, the
dream of a united national community, conferring on
all a sense of belonging and participation and being
cared for. In practice, of course, things work out quite
differently. Its schemes of social belonging usually end
up with populations far too accustomed to receiving
and demanding. Those most skilled at mobilizing
demands fare best. While social democracy speaks

the language of community and compassion and caring, the reality is original sin, that is, socialized self-interest. Social democratic societies are not notably happy or contented societies.

In the social democratic context, a stakeholder is a claimant on the public purse. From a social democratic perspective, the stakeholder in the traditional sense, the true owner and bearer of responsibility and risk, is called a "mere shareholder" and is accused of having a "pinched," "narrow," and "selfish" view of society. To paraphrase George Santayana on Puritans, a social democrat cannot bear to see self-reliant, responsible, prospering, and independent institutions without wanting to put them in state-directed harness.

The paradox of socialism is that it actually results in the opposite of its hopes: an unparalleled isolation of individuals from the bonds of personal responsibility and social cooperation.[24] In an obverse paradox, while extolling the language of community and social sharing, social democracy necessarily excites envy, a social passion worse than hatred, and it inevitably divides citizens into factions that make on the state unceasing claims of favor, entitlement, and privilege. Each faction jealously and militantly claims its own "just" stake. Thus, social democracy dampens ambition, imagination, personal independence, individual risk taking, and economic creativity; it nourishes a society of clients, supplicants, and demanders of rewards; and it aspires to a relative uniformity of condition among those whose stakeholding amounts to what Hayek aptly called serfdom. Eight score years ago Tocqueville also foresaw this effect:

I am trying to imagine under what novel fea-
tures despotism may appear in the world. In
the first place, I see an innumerable multitude of men, alike and equal, constantly cir-
cling around in pursuit of the petty and ba-
nal pleasures with which they glut their
souls. . . . Over this kind of men stands an
immense, protective power which is alone
responsible for securing their enjoyment and
watching over their fate. That power is abso-
lute, thoughtful of detail, orderly, provident,
and gentle. It would resemble parental au-
thority if, father-like, it tried to prepare its
charges for a man's life, but on the contrary,
it only tries to keep them in perpetual child-
hood. . . . It gladly works for their happi-
ness but wants to be sole agent and judge of
it. It provides for their security, foresees and
supplies their necessities, facilitates their pleasures, manages their principal concerns, di-
rects their industry, makes rules for their tes-
taments, and divides their inheritances. Why
should it not entirely relieve them from the
trouble of thinking and all the cares of living?[25]

That is not a stakeholding society. That is serfdom.

The End of the Republican Experiment?

As the first streaking fingers of the twenty-first century rise toward dawn, there is no guarantee that the
republican experiment will not perish from the face
of the earth. The dream of social democracy, which
would replace the republican idea, still bewitches
many minds. Social democrats today claim to be con-

verted to markets, private property, and contemporary (rather than nineteenth-century Marxist) economics. But of course they mean *bridled* markets, *socially responsible* private property, and *government-
managed* economics. As Will Hutton puts it:
"Keynesian economics is best."[26] They cling to their
dream; it assures them of moral standing, indeed su-
periority.

In the American republic, both the economy and
religion are purposefully kept separate from the state.
Yet there is no way to keep the wall of separation between economy and state as high as it is between
church and state; this is so for two reasons. First, al-
though the supply of money could theoretically and
advantageously be privatized, as Friedrich Hayek[27]
has urged, we have long lived under a consensus that
the government, through the relatively independent
Federal Reserve Board, ought to maintain public control over money. Second, the workings of business,
founded on private contracts under the rule of law,
demand the involvement of government in the making and enforcement of corporate law.

But this asymmetry between religion, in which
"Congress shall make no law," and business, to which
the making and enforcing of law are indispensable,
makes it even more important for business leaders to
be philosophically vigilant—that is, *principled* and un-
relenting against the trespasses of government power
on private property.

At this point, commercial habits such as a mere
deal making and a mutually agreeable pragmatism
are self-mutilating. Business leaders must be careful
not to give away the store—and they must insist on

deadly seriousness in the use of key words such as *stakeholder*.

Will Hutton, for example, proposes eight major changes in British law, mandating eight sets of controls on procedures of corporate governance.[28] What he cannot stand is the firm's independence: "The firm is a law unto itself, sovereign of all it surveys. Its only job is to succeed in the market place." He makes "succeed in the marketplace" seem easy, trivial, frivolous—when British firms, like all others, are struggling to survive in global competition. And he makes even a limited sovereignty over oneself (under "the laws of nature and nature's God")—that is, liberty understood as self-government—seem like an abuse rather than the inner dynamism and goal of all human history.[29] Hutton takes no count, finally, of the burdens his eight proposals would pile onto the already inadequate shoulders of the regulatory bureaucracy, and no count whatever of the costs in animal spirits, inefficiency, bureaucratic overlay, excessive record keeping, poor morale, and feelings of pointlessness his "reforms" would entail.

His American counterparts are worse. Professor Ralph Estes, American University proponent of the Stakeholder Alliance and author of *Tyranny of the Bottom Line: Why Corporations Make Good People Do Bad Things*, also thinks keeping a sound bottom line is easy, so he wants to add a dozen or so other lines. For him, stakeholders "include employees, customers, neighbors and communities, financial investors, suppliers, and the greater society." Not just the Great Society, note, "the *greater* society"—"all who are affected significantly by the enterprise." Are all these persons to be asked to pay the corporation for tangential benefits they receive from it? Oh no. They are supposed to exact new costs from it:

> The scorecard has to be enlarged to incorporate effects on all stakeholders. It must record the workplace injuries, pollution emissions, product liability claims and settlements, recent layoff and plant closure data, indictments, fines by and settlements with government regulators. Indeed, it must record the information necessary for stakeholders to make informed decisions in the marketplace, the way the 1930s securities acts required reports that would permit financial investors to make informed decisions. And this information must be publicly available, in an annual Corporate Report to Stakeholders supplemented as necessary by ad hoc disclosures. With disclosure, stakeholders have the information they require to make informed economic decisions and can then regulate corporate behavior.[30]

American Labor Secretary Robert Reich, for a time the voice of Europe in America, also hectored corporate leaders, proposing the use of tax favors to steer corporations in directions social democrats favor.[31]

As the strongest private institutions standing in the way of the administrative state, business corporations are certain to be the unceasing target of the frustrated and almost desperate energies of the Left. Nearly all welfare states are broke or in most serious deficit. Many dependent populations are demoralized and living half lives rather worse in matters of the spirit than those of earlier generations of the poor (among whom so many of us were born), who at least felt independent and proud. In improving the lot of the elderly and in some forms of social insurance, the welfare state has had some sound successes that the party of liberty ought not to disparage but to defend. Nonetheless, in all the giant administrative states in our time, the new soft despotism has been experienced long enough and is coming to be hated.

In this age in which the welfare state is broke and in deficit, where then will the social democrats turn for plunder? The famous Willie Sutton robbed banks because that's where the money was; that, apparently, is where his near-namesake Will Hutton got the idea—in Hutton's case, not robbing banks but business corporations. He wants to leave their private property, risk taking, and free markets intact— only to regulate them, harness them, and guide them so his team gets the fruits they want, willy-nilly. (See the appendix.)

It is time, then, for public enemy number one, the business corporation, to take account of its own identity, its essential role in the future of self-governing republics, and its central position in the building of the chief alternative to government: civil society. The corporation is what it is and does what it does; but it is an invention of free people, not a cold meteor fallen from the skies. It has changed often in history and, by its very self-discipline, inventiveness, and creativity, has surmounted even greater threats than it faces today. Now, however, it will need a greater degree of philosophical and public policy self-consciousness than ever before. The corporation has some serious external enemies and some serious internal flaws—for example, in the procedures that lead to excessive compensation at the top, to excessive insecurity at all levels, to anomalies of self-governance, to turmoil about patents. The business corporation is once again in a fight for its life, and the sooner the dangers that menace it are exactly discerned, the better.

Next autumn, two more lectures are to follow this one, so please consider this first one a version of that old, famous telegram: "DISASTER STOP LETTER FOLLOWS."

The Legend of the Bay Steed

Once upon a time in Italy, a knight who had been gravely wounded returned home on his sturdy bay warhorse, a beautiful steed whose prancing and snorting, rearing and pawing the air thrilled all the children in the village. Everyone, man and woman alike, admired the beautiful bay. All said that he was the strongest horse they had ever seen. For *Il Re Arturo*—such was his name, an English name, the knight told them, to honor the Knights of the Round Table—not only carried the knight in all his heavy armor with ease; occasionally the brave steed, with the gravely wounded knight's permission, also pulled heavy loads that no other beast in the village could haul.

The wounded knight strictly forbade the townspeople from interfering with the freedom of the horse throughout most of the day. It is important, he said, for the steed to feed quietly and gambol at will around the meadow in which he is fenced.

Later that spring the knight died, and the townspeople inherited the horse and took him under common ownership. They congratulated themselves on all the great tasks they would have *Il Re Arturo* perform for them. One had boulders to remove from his fields. Another had the stumps of two great oaks, partially severed at the roots, to pull free from the earth and drag away. Others had other tasks.

Led by the mayor of the village, in consultation with the priest, the townspeople resolved that each household could use the great bay equally with every other, but whichever household used him that day must feed him that morning and that night. Further, each household must promise to allow him to be free during the height of the day, just as the knight always did, to maintain the steed's spirit and strength.

On the first day, Signor Barone took the steed to move his boulders. He began to feed the horse, but then noting how hot the morning sun already was, decided to hurry him into the field. "He will eat extra tonight," he said. Dragging the boulders took longer than expected, and *Il Re Arturo* got no time to rest—or replenish his spirit—until nearly 4 p.m. At that hour, the horse was bathed in sweat and too fatigued to eat. S. Barone shrugged his shoulders, and said that S. Bucelli would certainly rest the horse on the morrow.

S. Bucelli came early for the horse the next morning, however, and became annoyed because the great steed seemed listless and weary. "It's too early in the day for a great horse like you to be weary," he said. "A little social discipline will straighten you out." He whipped the horse, lightly at first, but more impatiently as the day wore on. After all, the horse was hauling logs to be cut for the village school, an important social project if there ever was one. Thinking that S. Barone must have fed the horse well the night before—"That's probably why he was reluctant to work this morning," Bucelli told himself, "He ate too much," so he fed him only handfuls of oats that night.

On Wednesday, Scarpignato took the horse, and on Thursday, Biaggio; Piccone on Friday; Mastrolilli on Saturday, and on Sunday Padre Umberto rode *Il Re Arturo* over the mountain to say a second Mass at the next village, whose pastor was away visiting his sick mother in another town. Padre Umberto noted that the beautiful horse seemed slow and tired, but he attributed it to the hard climb up the mountain, and the steep descent.

Each day *Il Re Arturo* grew thinner. He was never bathed. No one rubbed down his coat. Each person in the village, knowing how much everybody loved and admired *Il Re Arturo*, assumed that the others were feeding him lavishly. Actually, he was given very little, and never the good grains.

By the end of the summer, *Il Re Arturo* was plainly languishing, grew ill, and died. The village gave him a noble burial. They praised him and all said how much they loved him, and how much he had contributed to the city. Most of their high hopes, of course, now went unfulfilled. They had barely begun the long list of tasks they had first imagined accomplishing. They would accomplish those on the morrow, they said, on some coming lucky morrow, when another gift like *Il Re Arturo* would descend unbidden upon them. They all attributed the good steed's death to grief for his fallen master, the noble knight, whose generosity to the village they vowed never to forget.

They tell the story of the beautiful and powerful horse still today. *Il Re Arturo* grows stronger and more beautiful in every telling.[32]

Notes

1. As the doyen of American Marxist historians wrote in 1990, "Less than seventy-five years after it officially began, the contest between capitalism and socialism is over: capitalism has won." Robert Heilbroner, "Was the Right Right All Along?" *Harper's*, January 1991, p. 18.

2. Early on, Hutton indicates the thinkers in the American tradition whom he considers allies: John Kenneth Galbraith, Robert Reich, and Lester Thurow. See Will Hutton, *The State We're In* (London: Jonathan Cape, 1995), p. xi.

3. *Newsweek*, February 26, 1996, pp. 44–51.

4. Alan MacFarlane, *The Culture of Capitalism* (London: Blackwell, 1987), p. 189.

5. All but approximately 44,000 of these firms employ fewer than 20 persons. All figures in this and the next paragraph are from *Statistical Abstract of the United States 1995* (Washington, D.C.: U.S. Department of Commerce, 1996).

6. An important note: Since in many cities great new hospital facilities, with their attendant research institutes, are now the single largest employer, and since some state universities have more employees than even the largest business corporations in their states, the number and type of entities covered by the terms *corporate law, corporate governance*, and even *business corporation* are quite vast. Not all hospital complexes these days, for example, are nonprofits. But even the so-called nonprofits actually need to budget each year for future improvements and new

technologies and therefore must operate with an annual excess of income over existing costs; this is very like a profit margin. And in not a few of their activities these days, universities are divided into what are, in effect, profit centers.

7. Paul Johnson further states, "The transformation took place when the Benedictine or Benedictine-type rule was grafted on to earlier forms. Thus the foundation at Fontanelle on the banks of the lower Seine, near Rouen . . . became a major agricultural colony after adopting a regular discipline in the mid-seventh century." Paul Johnson, *A History of Christianity* (New York: Atheneum, 1980), pp. 148–49.

8. See Luigi Sturzo, *Church and State*, 1 (Notre Dame: University of Notre Dame, 1962), pp. 36–37. Another account is given by Newman C. Eberhardt, C.M., *A Summary of Catholic History, Vol. I: Ancient and Medieval History* (St. Louis: B. Herder Book Co., 1961), pp. 163–64.

9. Friedrich A. Hayek, *New Studies in Philosophy, Politics and Economics* (London: Routledge & Kegan Paul, 1978), p. 260.

10. Kazua Noda, "The Corporation," *The New Encyclopaedia Britannica*, Macropaedia, 5 (Chicago: H.H. Benton, 1977), p. 183.

11. In the first of his 1959 Wabash lectures on economics and freedom, the historian Jacob Viner noted: "It was a commonplace of Greek and Roman thought, destined to be absorbed in the Christian tradition, that trade was either by its inherent nature, or through the temptations it offered to those engaged in it, pervasively associated with fraud and cheating, especially, according to Cicero, if it were 'small,' or retail trade." Jacob Viner, *Essays on the Intellectual History of Economics*, ed. D. Irwin (Princeton: Princeton University Press, 1991), p. 39.

12. See my *Business as a Calling* (New York: Free Press, 1996).

13. Oscar Handlin, "The Development of the Corporation," in *The Corporation: A Theological Inquiry*, ed. M. Novak and J. Cooper (Washington, D.C.: AEI Press, 1981), p. 10.

14. Ibid., p. 10: "They were not all going somewhere. But some of them were; and they permitted the penetration of areas even before the passengers and the freight they would carry appeared. In the same way, a whole series of new economic opportunities were able to be exploited at the end of the century because the device of the corporation permitted the rapid mobilization of large amounts of capital, of managerial ability, and of the enterprise to bring these processes to a successful conclusion."

15. Ibid., p. 2.

16. Oakeshott defined the "enterprise association" as a "relationship in terms of the pursuit of some common purpose, some substantive condition of things to be jointly procured, or some common interest to be continuously satisfied." This was to distinguish it from a "civil association," rule-governed but not focused on particular ends. See Michael Oakeshott, *On Human Conduct* (Oxford: Oxford University Press, 1975), p. 114.

17. Peter Drucker, *The Concept of the Corporation* (New York: The John Day Co., 1946), pp. 20–21.

18. Tocqueville wrote:

> While the law allows the American people to do everything, there are things which religion prevents them from imagining and forbids them to dare. Religion, which never intervenes directly in the government of American society, should therefore be considered as the first of their political institutions, for although it did not give them the taste of liberty, it singularly facilitates their use thereof.

Alexis de Tocqueville, *Democracy in America*, ed. J.P. Mayer, trans. G. Lawrence (New York: Anchor Books, 1966), p. 292.

19. In Hamilton's words,

> It has been frequently remarked that it seems to have been reserved to the people of this country, by their conduct and example, to decide the important question, whether societies of men are really capable or not of establishing good government from *reflection* and *choice* or whether they are forever destined to depend for their political constitutions on accident and force. [Emphasis added.]

Alexander Hamilton, James Madison, and John Jay, *The Federalist Papers*, intro. by C. Rossiter (New York: New American Library, 1961), p. 33.

20. The phrase "commercial republic" was first developed by Montesquieu, in trying to understand why England, the nation of shopkeepers and property owners, seemed in all Europe to be so well governed and her manners so agreeable. The concept was well argued over by the founders, as in *Federalist* No. 6, and formed the backbone of the tradition called "commercial republicanism" and "civic republicanism" here and "civic humanism" by Adam Smith in Scotland. See Ralph Lerner, "Commerce and Character: The Anglo-American as New-Model Man," in Ralph Lerner, *The Thinking Revolutionary: Principle and Practice in the New Republic* (Ithaca, N.Y.: Cornell University Press, 1987), pp. 185–221; see also John Robertson, "Adam Smith as Civic Moralist," in *Wealth and Virtue: The Shaping of Political Economy in the Scottish Enlightenment*, ed. Istvan Hont and Michael Ignatieff (Cambridge: Cambridge University Press, 1983), pp. 179–202.

21. See Baron De Montesquieu, *The Spirit of the Laws*, translated by T. Nugent (New York: Macmillan, 1949), Book xx, chaps. 1, 2, 7, 8.

22. Jerry Ellis, Joint Economic Committee, 104th U.S. Congress, "We Have Met the Corporations and They Us," unpublished working paper proposed for the JEC, 104th Congress, 1996.

23. See William Safire's "On Language," *New York Times Magazine*, May 5, 1996, pp. 26–27.

24. See Giovanni Sartori, "The Market, Planning, Capitalism and Democracy," *This World*, vol. 5 (Spring/Summer 1983), pp. 68–71.

25. Tocqueville, *Democracy in America*, pp. 691–92.

26. Hutton, *The State We're In*, chap. 9.

27. Hayek outlined his proposal for the privatization of money in *The Denationalization of Money* (London: Institute of Economic Affairs, 1978).

28. Hutton writes:

> There are . . . no legal requirements for audit committees to provide alternative sources of financial information to the non-executive directors. There are no independent remuneration committees to assess directors' pay. There is no system for ensuring that the custodians of company pension funds are independent. Firms do not have to establish supervisory boards to monitor the performance of their executive board as they do in Europe; rather the board is judge and jury of its own performance. There is no formal incorporation of key stakeholders—trade unions and banks—in the constitution of the firm. There is no obligation to establish works councils or to recognise trade unions as partners in the enterprise. The public cannot easily obtain company information. Transparent and commonly accepted accounting guidelines are not enforced, and can vary hugely from firm to firm or from year to year; the annual report and accounts

set out precisely what the board and its chairman decide they will set out. The firm is a law unto itself, sovereign of all it surveys. Its only job is to succeed in the marketplace.

Hutton, *The State We're In*, p. 295.

29. One may speak of "sovereignty of the self" when one means self-government with reference to other human beings—the sense in which citizens of the United States are "sovereign citizens," able to act as "We the People" in erecting a government based on their consent. Face to face with God, the governor of our autonomy, we are subjects, not sovereigns. This is the sense in which we say that it is the truth that makes us free; "And ye shall know the truth, and the truth shall make you free" (John 8:32).

30. Ralph Estes, "Antidote to Economic Anxiety," *Washington Post*, May 19, 1996.

31. Reich, in a February 6, 1996, speech at George Washington University, "Pinkslips, Profits, and Paychecks: Corporate Citizenship in an Era of Smaller Government," emphasized the "narrow economic calculus" that motivates corporations and proposed the following:

If we want companies to do things which do not necessarily improve the returns to shareholders but which are beneficial for the economy and society as a whole ... we have to give business an economic reason to do so. One possibility would be to reduce or eliminate corporate income taxes only for companies that achieve certain minimum requirements along these dimensions.

Quoted in Joint Economic Committee, 104th U.S. Congress, "Corporate Responsibility or Company Store? Secretary Reich's Regressive Proposal," February 1996.

32. An invention of mine, based on a fifteenth-century fable told by St. Bernardine of Siena, Italy. For more

on St. Bernardine's economic thinking, see Alejandro A. Chafuen, *Christians for Freedom: Late Scholastic Economics* (San Francisco: Ignatius Press, 1986), and "What St. Bernardin's Ass Could Teach the Bishops," *Reason* (August/September, 1987), pp. 43–46.

About the Author

MICHAEL NOVAK, the Templeton laureate, holds the George Frederick Jewett Chair in Religion, Philosophy, and Public Policy at the American Enterprise Institute. He is also AEI's director of social and political studies. In 1986, Mr. Novak headed the U.S. delegation to the Conference on Security and Cooperation in Europe. In 1981 and 1982, he led the U.S. delegation to the United Nations Human Rights Commission in Geneva. In 1994, Mr. Novak won the Templeton Prize for Progress in Religion, the Wilhelm Weber Prize, and the International Award of the Institution for World Capitalism. The author of more than twenty-five books, he is also a cofounder and former publisher of *Crisis* and has been a columnist for both *National Review* and *Forbes*.

www.ingramcontent.com/pod-product-compliance
Lightning Source LLC
Jackson TN
JSHW011943131224
75386JS00041B/1542